Entrepreneur.
kids

Launch Your Own Business

By the Staff of Entrepreneur Media

Entrepreneur
PRESS.

T0125833

Entrepreneur Press, Publisher
Consulting Editor: Michelle Martinez
Cover Design: Andrew Welyczko
Production and Composition: AbandonedWest Creative, Inc.

An application to register this book for cataloging has been submitted to the Library of Congress.

ISBN 978-1-64201-140-1 (paperback) | ISBN 978-1-61308-453-3 (ebook)

Printed in the United States of America

25 24 23 22 21 10 9 8 7 6 5 4 3 2 1

References

Deeb, George. "Top 5 Lessons From a Kid Entrepreneur (Pay Attention, Public Schools!)." *Entrepreneur Magazine*, Irvine, CA. https://www.entrepreneur.com/article/350052

MacQuarrie, A.J. "8 Tips for Entrepreneurial High School Students Ready to Start Their First Business." *Entrepreneur Magazine*, Irvine, CA. https://www.entrepreneur.com/article/300403

Rampton, John. "What You Can Learn From 8 Kids Already Making a Million Dollars." *Entrepreneur Magazine*, Irvine, CA. https://www.entrepreneur.com/article/241189

Staff of Entrepreneur Media. *SYOB: Start Your Own Business*, 7th Edition. Entrepreneur Press, Irvine, CA.

Image Credits

Entrepreneur kids

Contents
launch your own business

**Get Ready To Be
An Entrepreneur** 2

What Are Your Goals? 4
Let's Make Some Goals WRITING 6

It's All About Timing 8
Time For A Business 9
Business Smarts 10
Can You Crack
The Business Code? PUZZLE 11
Entrepreneur Word Search PUZZLE 12

Let's Get Started 13
Dreaming About
Your Business WRITING 15
Brainstorm Your Business
Ideas WRITING 16

Is Your Idea A Good One? ... 17

It's All About Customers 18
Let's Find Your Customers WRITING 19

Market Research 20
Namestorming WRITING 21

The Business Plan 22
Sample Business Plan 23
Write Your Own
Business Plan WRITING 25
Design Your Own Logo 28
Design Your Own Business Card 29

All About Entrepreneurship
Crossword PUZZLE 30
Complete The Story:
Business "Cents" PUZZLE 31

All About Financing 32
The Candle-Making Business 33
The Tutoring Business 34
Your Business 35
Dreaming About A Mentor WRITING 37
Find The Message In The
Broken Words PUZZLE 38
Financing Smarts 39

**Meet The Entrepreneur:
Brendan Cox** 42

The Financing Word Search PUZZLE 45
Starting A Business Maze PUZZLE 46

**All About Marketing
And Advertising** 47
Creating A Headline 50
Design Your Own Advertisement 52
Marketing Smarts 53
Dreaming About Advertising WRITING .. 54
Find The Hidden Message PUZZLE 55

**Advice From Kid Entrepreneurs
Who've Made Over...
A Million Dollars!** 56

Launching A Business Resources 58
Puzzle Solutions 59

GET READY TO BE AN *entrepreneur*

What Is an **Entrepreneur?**

An entrepreneur is someone who has an idea for a business and starts the business even though they may lose money. Most entrepreneurs dream big—they see great possibilities where others do not. Entrepreneurs are passionate about a product or an idea and are willing to take financial risks to make their dream a reality. And most importantly, entrepreneurs are confident people who are not afraid to fail because sometimes it takes more than one try to have a successful business.

Anyone who wants to be an entrepreneur can become one. It doesn't mean you have to become one right now, but the first step to becoming an entrepreneur is to think about it! Imagine what your life would be like if you were to start your own business. Does being in charge of a company excite you? Do you want to be your own boss? Many entrepreneurs start more than one business over their lifetime. In fact, most entrepreneurs will tell you that they started many different kinds of businesses as kids. It's not just a way to make money; it's a way to find out more about yourself!

Do You Have What It Takes to Be an Entrepreneur?

It's rare that one person has all the qualities needed to be successful in business. Everyone has strong and weak points. What's important is to understand your strengths and weaknesses. Are you friendly? Are you a hard worker? Are you well-organized?

So, what does it take to be an entrepreneur? It takes a lot of hard work. Starting a new business on your own can be rewarding, but it can also be frustrating if things don't turn out the way you want them to. Whatever you do, don't give up. Keep trying your ideas, and chances are, something will work out. ⓚ

WHAT ARE YOUR goals?

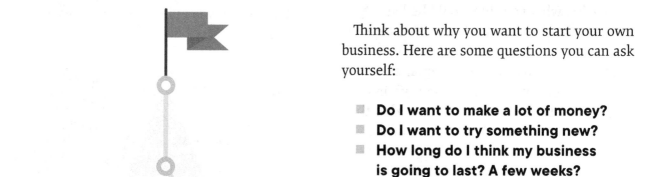

Think about why you want to start your own business. Here are some questions you can ask yourself:

- **Do I want to make a lot of money?**
- **Do I want to try something new?**
- **How long do I think my business is going to last? A few weeks? Months? Years?**
- **Is my business going to help people?**
- **Am I going to sell a product (like jewelry) or offer a service (like dog walking)?**

Setting goals not only gives you a road map for success, but it also shows you the other things you could do if you need to make a change along the way.

Did You Know?

Researcher Phillippa Lally published a study in the *European Journal of Social Psychology* that says it takes an average of 66 days to form a new habit.

When you think about your goals, make sure you keep a positive attitude. It's also important to set realistic goals. If you set a goal to make $100,000 a month, that goal is probably unrealistic. Start with small steps, such as making an extra $25 every week. Once your first goal is met, you can aim for larger ones.

You should also set both short- and long-term goals. A **short-term goal** is one that you can complete quickly like keeping your room clean for a month or saving money every week by making your lunch instead of buying it. A

Did You Know?

If you say your goal out loud each day to remind yourself of what you are working for, you are more likely to meet your goal. Repeating your goal to yourself helps you remember it.

long-term goal can take months or years, like saving to buy a car when you're 16. Short-term goals are easier to meet than long-term goals. Ⓚ

LET'S MAKE SOME *goals*

Setting goals gives you an ongoing roadmap for success. Make sure you review your goals every so often. Reviewing your goals every week or every month will help keep you on track to meeting them.

So, let's get started!

1 **I Want to Start My Own Business** Because...

2 **What I Think** I Will Like Best **About Starting My Own Business Is...**

Did You Know?

If you say your goal out loud each day to remind yourself of what you are working for, you are more likely to meet your goal. Repeating your goal to yourself helps you remember it.

Did You Know?

Benjamin Franklin is considered America's first entrepreneur. In addition to running his own printing press and newspaper, Franklin is also credited with starting the first library!

3 My Business Is Going to Help Others By...

4 In Three Months, I Would Like My Business To Be...

5 The Most Important Part of My Business Will Be...

IT'S ALL ABOUT *timing*

Starting a business takes time. Think about your current schedule. Between school, homework, and activities, do you have time to start a business? Start by making a list of all the things you need to do. Then map out a schedule of what your week looks like. Here's an example:

Emma is in school Monday through Friday. She also has swim practice on Tuesdays and Thursdays. Other than swimming and homework, she doesn't have any other commitments. She could work on her new business on Mondays, Wednesdays, Fridays, and the weekends. It looks like Emma has the time to get started on her new business! ⓚ

Emma's Schedule

DAY	SCHEDULE
Monday	8:00–3:00 School 3:30–4:30 Homework 6:30–8:30 Open
Tuesday	8:00–3:00 School 3:30–5:00 Swim Practice 5:00–6:00 Dinner 6:00–7:00 Homework
Wednesday	8:00–3:00 School 3:30–4:30 Homework 6:30–8:30 Open

DAY	SCHEDULE
Thursday	8:00–3:00 School 3:30–5:00 Swim Practice 5:00–6:00 Dinner 6:00–7:00 Homework
Friday	8:00–3:00 School 3:30–4:30 Homework 6:30–8:30 Open
Saturday & Sunday	Open

Time For A Business

Now let's see how much time you have to start your own business. Use the template below to write down your typical weekly schedule.

DAY	WHAT DO YOU HAVE TO DO EACH DAY?
Monday	
Tuesday	
Wednesday	
Thursday	
Friday	
Saturday	
Sunday	

BUSINESS
smarts

What Does It Mean to Be Productive?

If you can get a lot of things done in a day and manage your time, you are **productive**. If you are going to start your own business, being productive is a must! There are many different tools to help you be productive. Using a calendar to schedule your time or making a "to-do" list are great ways to help you be productive.

What Is an Investor?

An **investor** is someone who has money to put into your business. For example, if you want to start a business selling bath bombs, but you don't have enough money to buy all the materials you need to make them, you could ask someone who does have the money to loan it to you. If this person chooses to give you the money, it will make them an investor in your business.

What Is a Franchise?

Think of a well-known fast-food company like McDonalds. Each McDonalds is part of a **franchise**, a business you can open and run that sells the company's products. To open a franchise, you have to pay a fee to the company, called a **franchise fee**, for the use of the company's logo. You will also have to offer the same products made the same way. You won't be able to start a franchise until you are an adult and have the money to buy one, but it can be a great opportunity to think about buying in your future.

What Does Risk vs. Reward Mean?

This is something that anyone thinking of starting a business needs to know. If you take a **risk**, you are taking a chance that something might not work out the way you hope. A **reward** is something you receive in return for doing a good job Is the risk of starting your own business worth the reward? What is the risk of your business failing? Will you lose money? Are you only risking the time you put into starting it? Once you know the risk, then the reward is its opposite. What is the reward of your business succeeding? Will you make a lot of money? Only you can decide if the risk of starting your own business is worth the reward. Ⓚ

business code?

Use the American Sign Language (ASL) alphabet below to translate the code.

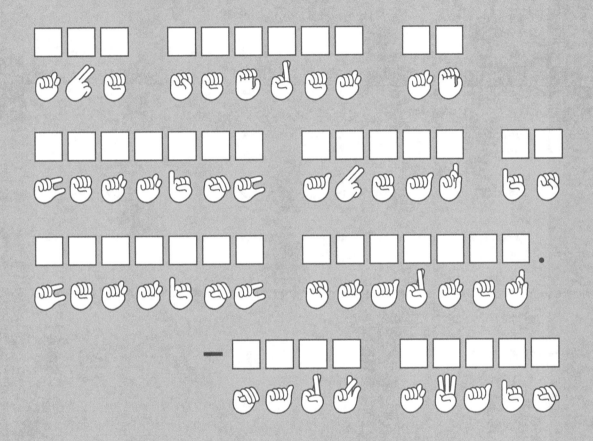

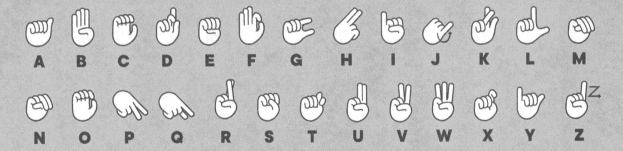

ANSWER KEY ON PAGE 59

ENTREPRENEUR
word search

Find the words that are hidden in the puzzle. Words may be forward, backward, horizontal, or vertical.

```
B W E G D R E A M F B E
L J N S G Q W P M M P S
L K T C N V N R R O O I
U S R H I L Y O O N S H
F I E E D M S D T E S C
S R P D E D S U S Y I N
S S R U A R E C E S B A
E L E L P A N T V O I R
C A N E B W I I N J L F
C O E D L E S V I Q I V
U G U O M R U E L S T Z
S S R N I D B Z H E Y B
```

ENTREPRENEUR
BUSINESS
SCHEDULE
DREAM

GOALS
IDEA
MONEY
PRODUCTIVE

SUCCESSFUL
RISK
FRANCHISE
INVESTOR

POSSIBILITY
REWARD

ANSWER KEY ON PAGE 59

LET'S GET started

Starting your business is hard work, fun, and exciting. There's never a dull moment. You can start a business at any time in your life. There's no time better than now to embark on the adventure of your life!

You know those ideas you've been thinking about? Write them down. What's your best one? What makes it better? How can you gain an edge? Talk about your idea with your friends and gather feedback from them, parents, teachers, and your target customers. Then for it. Don't make it complicated. Your business can be a simple one like babysitting, yard work, or dog walking.

Did You Know?

Thomas Edison is known for inventing the light bulb, but he also made over 1,000 different inventions!

Find a Mentor

Before you start your business, find a mentor, a trusted grownup who can give you advice. The business world is filled with people who've started their own businesses and want to pass along their knowledge, lessons, and insights. It might be scary to ask someone, but go ahead and approach some local business owners and ask them if they can help you. You will always need someone supportive and honest to turn to for advice.

Be Okay With Failure

Everyone fails. Our failures teach us what we need to be successful. Overcome any fear of failure you might feel—that feeling is the biggest obstacle of any you'll ever face. Try. Fail. Get back up. Learn from your failures. Did you need more focus, attention, or effort? Every failure is a chance to learn more about yourself.

Put Yourself Out There

When you start a business, you will meet a lot of new people. If you want to get better at

Keep Reading! ⟶

talking to new people, get out of your comfort zone. Run for student government or join a sports team or club. If you think of yourself as shy, get involved with theater. It can help you overcome shyness and you'll develop many skills like working with people. You can start getting comfortable with being a leader because that's what entrepreneurship is all about. You'll benefit from working on teams with others.

Recognize Opportunities

Look for a problem in your community. Think about how you can create a business around solving it. Start thinking about it even if you never do it. Start exercising the creative brainstorming part of your brain. Ⓚ

DREAMING ABOUT *your business*

If you could start and run any business you wanted, what would it be?
How much money would you make? What would you do with all of your money?

Brainstorm Your Business Ideas

List your business ideas. Choose a favorite.

....

....

....

What would you need to do to start this business?

....

....

....

How long do you think it will take to start this business?

....

....

....

How much money do you think you will need to start this business?

....

....

....

IS YOUR *idea* A GOOD ONE?

So, you've got an idea for a business. But is it a good one? If you can answer all three of these questions, great! If not, take some time to rework your idea.

❶ Does Your Business Solve a Problem?

Solving a problem means offering a solution to make people's lives easier. Pretend you want to start a dog washing business. Does this solve a problem? Will it make life easier for some people? Yes, because all dogs need a bath at some point and if your business is offering to do it for people, you will be saving them time.

❷ Can Your Business Grow or Be Expanded to Offer More Products or Services?

There are lots of ways to expand a dog washing business. You can include other services like trimming nails or brushing their teeth.

❸ Do People Want Your Product or Service?

Start testing your idea and talking about it with friends and family members. Are they as excited about your idea as you are? ❸

Did You Know?

The word **idea** comes from the Greek word *ennoia*, which originally meant "the act of thinking."

IT'S ALL ABOUT *customers*

Now that you have an idea for a business, you will need to figure out who your target market is. In this case, **target market** means who you are going to sell to. Who will be your customers? First, figure out if you will sell a **product** (an actual item you can hold in your hand) or a **service** (performing a task for someone else). In other words, are you going to sell something like bracelets or lemonade? Or are you going to sell a service like tutoring younger kids or mowing neighbors' lawns? Knowing whether you are selling a product or a service will help you figure out your target market. ⓚ

LET'S FIND YOUR

① Describe **Your Business Idea**

② **What Will Your Product/Service Be** Used For?

③ **Are There** Similar **Products/Sevices Out There?**

④ **How Are You** Different **From Your Competition?**

⑤ Who **Do You Want To Sell To?**

⑥ **How** Old **Are They? Are They Kids? Grownups?**

MARKET research

Now that you have an idea for a business and you know who your customers are going to be, you will need to do some research to see if there is a need for your product or service. This is called **market research** and big companies do it all the time. For example, if you live in an area where it snows, you could open up a business that provides the service of shoveling snow. Before you get started, you'll need to know if there are other local businesses that do this. If there are, is there enough of a demand for more than one business? How much money do similar businesses charge for this service?

No matter what type of business you want to start, chances are there is someone out there who has done something similar. Researching the businesses that are like yours will help you make your business more successful. Keep a notebook or a document on your computer with a list of businesses and write down how they are similar to your business and how they are different. Ⓚ

Namestorming

What's in a name? A lot, when it comes to small-business success! The right name can make your business the talk of the town. The wrong name can confuse people. You should put just as much effort into naming your business as you did into coming up with your idea. Finding a good business name can be hard. Some people think a good business name is clear and informative. If you're selling bath bombs and your name is Emma, call it "Emma's Bath Bombs." But what if your bath bomb business is a huge success and you decide to sell other things too, like shower bombs? Then "Emma's Bath Bombs" doesn't tell the whole story.

Begin brainstorming by looking in dictionaries, books, and magazines to get some ideas. Get friends and relatives to help—the more minds the better! There is no right or wrong way to name your business. Most importantly, it needs to be something you like!

Some Naming Tips

- **Choose a name that you like and that you think your customers will like.**

- **Keep it short! Don't choose a name that is too long or confusing. And stay away from puns that only you understand.**

- **Don't use the word "Inc." after your name unless your company is actually incorporated.**

LET'S *list them!*

Write down a few possible names for your business. Show your list to some of your family and friends. Which one do they like best?

1 . . . .

2 . . . .

3 . . . .

4 . . . .

Did You Know?

The word *market* has more than one meaning. A **market** is a place where people go to buy and sell things, like at a grocery store. The word *market* can also mean the way things are bought or sold. If someone says, "There is a **market** for children's shoes," what they mean is that there are many people who are interested in buying shoes, so a business selling them could be successful.

THE BUSINESS *plan*

Every successful business has a plan. When you're first starting out, your **business plan**, a written plan that shows how you will run your business, will help guide your decisions. Many big companies have very long and formal business plans. Often, these big companies use their business plans to show to banks or investors when they are hoping to borrow money.

So, what exactly is a business plan, and how do you put one together? There are three main parts to a business plan.

1 **The first part is where you talk about your business.** You should describe what it is, and how you plan to make it a success.

2 **The second part is where you talk about your potential customers.** Who are they? Why will they buy your product? This is also where you talk about your competition and how you think you can beat it.

3 **The last part is where you talk about money.** How much will it cost to start your business? How much of a profit do you think you will make? You may need help from a parent or other adult to help you think this section through.

Sample Business Plan

PART ❶
Describe Your Business

What kind of business do you want to start?

I am going to start a babysitting business. I will also be an agent for other babysitters so customers will only have to get in touch me. If I can't babysit for them, I will find another sitter who can.

What will the name of your business be?

The Babysitting Connection

Why do you think there is a need for this business?

Many people in my neighborhood hire babysitters to watch their children while they run errands or enjoy some free time.

How will people benefit from your business?

Parents only have to call one number to get a sitter. If I'm not available, I'll find someone who is. This way, parents don't have to call many people to find a sitter.

How will your business work? Will you have any help? Or are you the only one in your business?

Not only will I be a babysitter, but I will also help other babysitters get jobs. I will charge other babysitters a small fee for getting them the job.

PART ❷
Describe Your Customers and Competition

Who are your customers going to be, how old are they, and what are their interests?

My customers are parents in their 20s and 30s. I'm not sure what their interests are, but I know they love their children and are looking for a safe, reliable sitter.

Why are people going to buy your product or service?

I think people will use my service because it's easy to call one phone number to get a babysitter. Parents won't have to make several calls to find a sitter.

How is your business going to be different from other similar businesses?

I took a babysitting class so I am qualified to babysit. Plus, I am representing many other babysitters who have also taken a babysitting class. If I can't do the job, I can find someone else who can.

How much are your competitors charging?

Some agencies in my area charge $10 to $15 an hour.

Keep Reading! ⟶

Sample Business Plan

PART ❸
Describe Your Costs

Explain how you are going to make your product.

This doesn't apply to me because my business is a providing a service.

How much are you going to charge?

I will charge $8 an hour for one child, $12 for two, and $15 for three. If there are more than three children to watch, two babysitters will be needed.

How much money will the supplies to get you started cost?

I need $20 to print out flyers, and I need a reliable phone. I found a phone that costs $99 plus $69 a month. I already have a calendar, and can also use a free calendar app on the phone to schedule appointments.

How much money will you need to start your business? Do you have enough of your own money to get you started?

I need $188 to get started. I have half of the money in savings. I will need to talk to my parents about the phone and monthly fee.

How much money do you think you will make?

I think I'll be able to make about $100 a month.

write your own business plan

What kind of business do you want to start?

What will the name of your business be?

How much money will the supplies to get you started cost?

How will people benefit from your business?

How will your business work? Will you have any help?
Or are you the only one in your business?

Who are your customers going to be, how old are they, and what are their interests?

Why are people going to buy your product or service?

How is your business going to be different from other similar businesses?

How much are your competitors charging?

Explain how you are going to make your product.

How much are you going to charge?

Why do you think there is a need for this business?

How much money will you need to start your business?
Do you have enough of your own money to get you started?

How much money do you think you will make?

Many businesses have logos to make their business easily recognizable. A logo is a symbol that represents your company. Think of some logos that you've seen. Does your favorite T-shirt have a logo? What about your backpack? Or your favorite snack? There are different kinds of logos on all sorts of different products. What do you think your company's logo should look like? Draw your ideas below.

Business cards are small pieces of heavy paper with your business information printed on them. You can hand these out to customers. If you do a quick online search for business cards, you will find many examples and companies that will print business cards for you. Your business cards can be simple—just include your name, the name of your business, and a way to reach you. That could be via social media, email, or a phone number. Don't include your address unless you have a separate place for your business. Draw your ideas below.

MAX'S LAWN CARE

Lawn Mowing • Yard Clean Up • Flower Planting
Available On Weekends!

MAX'S LAWN CARE

Max Smith, Owner
Email: max@sample.com
Phone: (555)555-5555

Front

**Example
Card Design**

Back

ACROSS

4. Before starting a business, you should do ____ on it.
5. Some ____ is healthy for your business.
6. To achieve something is to have ____.
7. Selling a ____ means you are selling a product.
9. Selling a ____ means you are selling something that you do for someone else.

DOWN

1. A ____ is an item you sell to a customer.
2. A great ____ is the first step to starting a business.
3. Starting your own ____ is hard work!
5. Businesses need ____ in order to make money.
8. It can be really hard to think of a ____ for your business.

ANSWER KEY ON PAGE 59

business "cents"

Starting my first business was a _____ challenge.
ADJECTIVE

When I began _____ about what I _____ to do,
VERB   VERB

my _____ asked me to walk the _____ .
NOUN   NOUN

That gave me an idea! Maybe I could start a _____ business!
PHRASE

I began advertising my _____ business in my neighborhood.
NOUN

Boy, was I _____ after that! I walked _____ dogs,
NOUN   ADJECTIVE

_____ dogs, _____ dogs, and dogs so small they had
ADJECTIVE   ADJECTIVE

to be _____ . One thing I _____ , is that _____
VERB   VERB   NOUN

walking is a _____ business, but it's also _____ work!
ADJECTIVE   VERB

ALL ABOUT *financing*

Once you have decided on the type of business you want to start, the next step is to figure out how much money you are going to need to start and where you are going to get the money. Where you start depends on how much money you're going to need. Let's see how much starting your business is going to cost.

Cost

Remember how we talked about how there are two different kinds of businesses? There are businesses that make products and businesses that offer a service. If you are making a product, you are going to need more money up front than you will if you are offering a service because you have to make something. Here are two examples.

THE *candle-making* BUSINESS

Abby wants to start her own candle-making business. She's already made a couple of different candles from a kit she got for her birthday. She thinks she can sell them to her friends and family. She's going to start off by making 20 candles.

For Abby's business she is going to have *one-time expenses* and *recurring expenses*. **One-time expenses** are spent on items she's only going to need to buy once. These are things she can use over and over again, such as the melting pot for the wax to make her candles. **Recurring expenses** are items she's going to have buy over and over again to keep her business running, like the wax and wax sticks. If she's going to continue to sell candles, she's going to have to keep making them, which means buying more wax.

Abby has $100 of her own money that she wants to use toward her new business. How is she going to get the rest? Abby decides to show her parents her business plan so they can see she is serious about starting her own business.

Candle-Making Supplies	Cost	One-Time or Recurring
10 Pound Bag of Wax and Wax Sticks	$30.99	Recurring
20 Candle Tins	$16.99	Recurring
38 Fragrance Oils	$27.99	Recurring
1 Melting Pot	$29.99	One-Time
Dried Flowers	$19.99	Recurring
Labels for the candle tins	$5.99	Recurring
Costs	Total: $131.94	Recurring: $101.95

They decide to give her the rest of the money to start her business, but she is expected to pay them back once she makes enough money.

Keep Reading! ⟶

THE *tutoring* BUSINESS

Matthew is really good at math. He's always gotten good grades and likes to help his younger sister with her homework. His sister likes it when he helps her because he's always very patient and explains things in a way that she can understand. Matthew decides to start his own tutoring business.

Matthew's tutoring business isn't going to cost him a lot to start because he isn't selling a product. He wants to order business cards so he can pass them out to customers. Matthew has some money saved from his allowance so he can buy the business cards on his own. Although Matthew will need to order more business cards when he runs out, but he doesn't have to have them to run his business. So, they are not considered a recurring cost.

Tutoring Supplies	Cost	One-Time or Recurring
Business Cards	$10.99	One-Time
Costs	Total: $10.99	Recurring: $10.99

Profit

All successful businesses need to make a profit. A **profit** is the amount of money you make after you have paid for everything else. Have you ever heard the saying, "It takes money to make money?" What this means is that it takes money to start your business, so if you don't have any money, how are you going to start your business? Let's go back to Abby and her candle-making business. It's going to cost her $131.94 to start her business. In order for her to make a profit, she's going to need to make more than this.

Keep Reading! →

YOUR *supplies*

Think about the business you want to start. Are you selling a product or a service? What kinds of supplies will you need to get started and how much will they cost? Here's a template to help you get started.

Business Supplies	Cost	One-Time or Recurring
	$	
	$	
	$	
	$	
	$	
	$	
	$	
	$	
	$	
	$	
	$	
Costs	Total: $	Recurring: $

In addition to the amount of money that it will cost you to start your business, you also don't want to forget to pay yourself. You want to make money, right? We know that Abby needs to make at least $131.94 to make a profit, but what about all the time and effort Abby is going to put into making the candles? Plus, she's going to need to advertise her candles. All of this is going to take time. How much is Abby's time worth? Well, that's really up to Abby to decide. There is no right or wrong answer.

In order to come up with a price to charge for your product or service, think about both the amount of money it takes to start your business and the time it will take you to make the product. This is where you can use your math skills.

For example, Abby has enough materials to make 20 candles at a cost to her of $131.94—this means she will need to sell each candle for at least $6.60 in order to break even. **Breaking even** means she's only getting the initial amount of money back. She's not making a profit. If she wants to make a profit, she's going to need to sell her candles for more than $6.60 apiece. How much should she sell them for? Again, there is no right or wrong answer. When it is your business, you get to decide how much to charge for your product.

If Abby decides to sell her candles for $10 each, she will need to sell 13 to break even. The good thing about breaking even is that she won't lose any money and she will have enough to pay her parents back the money they loaned her. If she sells all 20, she'll make a profit of $68.06!

DREAMING ABOUT
a mentor

If you could have lunch with any entrepreneur, who would it be? What kind of business did they start? What kinds of questions would you ask them?

FIND THE MESSAGE IN THE
broken words

Unscramble the message by finding and placing the correct letter in each box. Try to guess the quote that is taking shape. For each set of rows, the missing letters you need to write into the blank boxes are listed below, but not in the correct order. The final message reads left-to-right, then down.

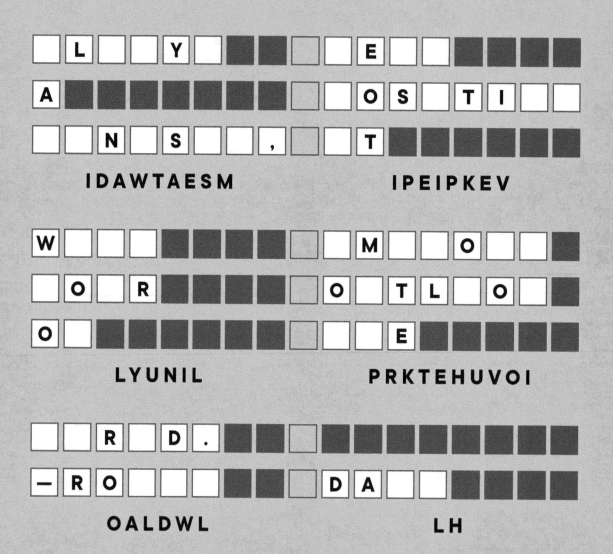

L   Y   E

A   O S   T I

  N S   ,   T

IDAWTAESM   **IPEIPKEV**

W   M   O

  O R   O T L   O

O   E

LYUNIL   **PRKTEHUVOI**

  R D.

— R O   D A

OALDWL   **LH**

ANSWER KEY ON PAGE 60

38   Entrepreneur **kids**

What are
Profit and Loss?

A **profit** is the amount of money you make once all of your bills are paid. **Loss** is the amount of money you are short once all of your bills are paid. For example, if you buy a pair of sunglasses for $10 and decide you don't really like them, you could sell them to a friend. If your friend pays you $12 for the sunglasses, then you just made a profit of $2! If your friend pays you $5 for the sunglasses, then you just took a loss of $5.

What Is a
Small Business Loan?

Many banks offer small business loans. A **small business loan** is an amount of money that a bank will give you to start your business. In order to get one of these loans, you have to fill out an application. You may also have to show them your business plan. It's not easy to get one of these loans for the first time. When a bank gives you a small business loan, you will have to pay them back. Usually there will be an agreed-upon amount you will have to pay them every month for a certain period of time.

Keep Reading! →

What Is a Financial Projection?

When you have your own business, a **financial projection** is how much you think your future earnings will be. There are a lot of ways that businesses come up with a financial projection. When you are just starting out, it can be hard to come up with a financial projection. To help you get started, you should keep track of all of your expenses and all of your earnings. After a couple of weeks, see how much money you've made. Have you made any? If you have made money, how much do you think you'll make in the next two weeks? More? Less? This will help you come up with a financial projection for the next few months of your business.

What Should I Do with the Money I Make from My Business?

Save it, of course! It's always a good idea to save some of your money. Try to save as much as you can—at least 20 percent of whatever you make. For example, if you make $100, put $20 in your savings. If you get in the habit of saving 20 percent of what you make, eventually you'll have enough money to buy something bigger like a game system, bike, or even a car!

After you save a portion of the money you make, you can **reinvest** some of your money back into your business, which means that you use the money for business purchases. If have $80 left over after saving some of your money, you can take part of that $80 and use it to buy more materials for the product you are selling or you can put it toward advertising materials. This way, you won't

have to borrow money from anyone else. Plus, if you use some money for advertising your business, you can get more customers and then continue to make more money.

Do I Have to Pay Taxes?

It all depends on how much you make. Rules on taxes are always changing, so it's best to ask the adults in your life. If you are only making a few hundred dollars ($600 or less), you probably won't need to pay taxes on it. However, if you are making a lot of money, chances are you will need to pay taxes. Ⓚ

Did You Know?

Starbucks is named after the character *Starbuck* in the book *Moby Dick* by Herman Melville.

MEET THE ENTREPRENEUR:
Brendan Cox

Brendan Cox is a 19-year-old entrepreneur who has founded 10 different successful businesses—starting at the age of 9. He has grown a $900 loan from his mother into $250,000 of profits today.

Brendan was a shy, eager, and creative kid in elementary school with a fascination for business and a drive to be successful (passed down by his father, who was his mentor). He was never interested in activities like playing video games, which he found boring. Instead, at an early age, he found creative ways to make money.

Inspired by his fascination with the DJ setups at a few family bat/bar-mitzvahs, his first business was a DJ company. He wanted to learn the business and taught himself how to mix music by conducting research on YouTube. After pitching this business idea to his parents, they agreed to help with funding for his equipment as a Christmas gift. He created business cards, flyers, and promotional products. Any money he made, he used to buy more equipment and lighting, party giveaways, and company gear he designed. He also hired another person to help him DJ.

By the time he entered middle school, Brendan lost his passion for entertainment, so he opened many new businesses including a social media management company, a phone cases business, a graphic design business, a teen odd jobs business and, most recently, a podcast for entrepreneurs called *All Up in Ur Business*.

Here are four pieces of advice from Brendan to young entrepreneurs.

❶ Raise Startup Money

"I was a 13-year-old kid with zero experience in the business world. I had to prove to my parents why they should trust me with their money. To do this, I created a PowerPoint presentation showing them my exact plan. This covered the breakdown of how I was going to spend the money and how I was going to earn the investment back, plus more. Don't assume just because they are your parents, they should just give you their hard-earned money."

❷ Get Adult Clients to Take You Seriously

"By learning how to talk and write in a professional manner, I limited situations where adults tried to negotiate prices or services. If you're unsure of how to respond or reach out to a person, always look up a template (template means "example") and make sure you use one that sounds professional, then personalize it for yourself. Always make sure there is confidence in your words. Confidence goes a long way in convincing others of quality service and experience."

Keep Reading! ⟶

"Always make sure there is confidence in your words. Confidence goes a long way in convincing others of quality service and experience."

> **"Keep yourself organized by making a calendar to space out blocks of time to determine what you need to accomplish in a day."**

❸ Juggle School and Work

"Keep yourself organized by making a calendar to space out blocks of time to determine what you need to accomplish in a day. Eliminate distractions you aren't gaining value from. An example of this is social media; so many kids waste hours a day on various platforms. If you are serious about your business, delegate that wasted time to improving your business."

❹ Make Your Brand Look Professional

"The key to having people take you seriously is making your self-image professional. Make sure you understand that your image on social media can be a dealbreaker. Across all social media platforms, I've had to change from being your average teen to becoming a professional. From having a professional picture to posting content that's relevant to your business, it all makes a difference. This also means making sure any information about you or your company sounds professional by using proper grammar and punctuation." ❿

You can read the full interview with Brendan at **entrepreneur.com/article/350052**.

THE FINANCING
word search

Find the words that are hidden in the puzzle. Words may be forward, backward, horizontal, vertical, or diagonal.

```
A H J E T A E R C Z O S
G N I T E K R A M L Q A
L L E S N Y B R G O R S
I N R A B Z O U A G Y R
N L M F W V L L G O O D
R E M O T S U C P K Z V
F N A L P A J Y I M T D
A P R O D U C T G X E F
Q C O M P E T I T I O N
H Z H C R A E S E R R Q
G Q K Y N A P M O C V U
S E I L P P U S K R O W
```

EMPLOYEE
PLAN
LOGO
MARKETING

SELL
CREATE
RESEARCH
WORK

CUSTOMER
NAME
COMPANY
GOOD

PRODUCT
COMPETITION
SUPPLIES

ANSWER KEY ON PAGE 60

Jack wants to start his own business mowing lawns, but he doesn't know how to get started. Help Jack get through the maze so he can start his own business!

ANSWER KEY ON PAGE 60

Entrepreneur kids

ALL ABOUT marketing AND advertising

Marketing and advertising help people know your business exists. What is the difference between marketing and advertising? **Marketing** is the process of finding out who your customers are and what their needs are. **Advertising** is the actual process of making your customers aware of your product. Advertising doesn't have to mean making a million-dollar TV commercial. There are lots of ways to advertise your business that are affordable or even free.

Keep Reading! →

Did You Know?

Coca-Cola makes so many different drinks that if you drank a different one every day it would take you 9 years to try all of them!

Create a Marketing Plan

Besides creating a business plan, you also need to create a marketing plan. A **marketing plan** is a written plan that tells how you will find and keep your customers. It includes information on what you sell, who will buy it, and what you will do to get customers.

Think about who your ideal customer would be. Let's say you want to start a pet-sitting service. How old are your customers? Where do they live? How often will they use your service? You may already know the answer to these questions—they're old enough to drive, they live in your neighborhood, they will use your service regularly if they have pets and they go out of town or to work.

It's important to have this information because it will help you decide how to advertise your business. If you are only going to work in your neighborhood, then you don't need to advertise outside of your neighborhood.

Once you know who your customers are going to be, you need to think about the best way to get their attention. How do you advertise to them? What would they like to see or read? Should you make flyers? Should you put up posters? Should you email them? Should you create a website? What are some ways you could get them to notice your business and either buy your product or use your service?

LET'S
list them!

List four ways you could advertise to your customers.

1 . . . .

2 . . . .

3 . . . .

4 . . . .

Making Advertising Materials

Every business needs to advertise—whether you are advertising with flyers around your neighborhood or creating a website or using social media—you will need to create something to make others aware of your business. Here are five rules help you create advertisements that attract customers:

1. **Attract attention.** This seems obvious, but nothing else matters unless you can do this. And that means having a truly great headline along with a picture or illustration. Learn more about headlines on page 50.

2. **Appeal to customer needs.** An ad that tells readers how they'll benefit from your product or service is more likely to catch their interest.

3. **Explain why your business is the best.** In other words, explain why the customer should pick your business over the competition.

4. **Prove your business is the best.** You can do this with a message from someone who has purchased your product or service and loved it.

5. **Make your customers want to take action.** This means it should include something like a coupon or discount.

Remember, advertising can be a lot of fun. Be creative and have fun with your advertisements. It's okay to write something funny or clever. In fact, the advertisements that people remember the most are usually the ones that made them laugh!

Keep Reading! →

Did You Know?

When chewing gum ads started showing people chewing two pieces of gum at the same time, their sales doubled instantly because people who watched the ads also started chewing two pieces of a gum at the same time.

CREATING A *headline*

Whether you are going to pass out flyers, send out emails, or post to your social media account, you will need to write a headline. A **headline** is a set of descriptive words at the top of a piece of writing, set in larger font. When you look at an advertisement, the headline is the first thing you see. Your headline should be unusual or interesting enough to get someone's attention.

The whole point of an advertisement is to get people interested in your business. If your headline makes people want to continue to read the rest of your advertisement, then you've done a great job!

Examples of Headlines That Got Noticed

- "Why some foods explode in your stomach."

- "The one thing you need to do today to be happy."

- "Studying tricks that made me an A student."

- "Is your dog sad while you're at work all day?"

Create a Flyer

Creating a flyer is a great way to advertise your business. You can easily create your own flyer on paper or by using a computer program. Whichever way you decide to create your flyer, make sure you include:

- **Your attention-grabbing headline**
- **A short description of your business**
- **The name of your business**
- **Your contact information (phone, email address, website—remember, don't ever share your home address)**
- **How much your product or service costs**
- **The hours that your business works (if necessary)**

Make Your Own Website

Before you create your own website, make sure you ask permission from your grownups. If they give you the okay, then go for it! There are many free website builders online that will guide you through the process. When you are first starting out, you don't need many pages. You will need a homepage with your company's title and a short description of what you are selling. You could also have links to an About page and a page that lists pricing and information on how to order.

Create a Video for Social Media

There are tons of ways to make a video. If you have a smartphone, you can create short videos talking about your business. You can show your product or talk about the service you are providing. You can ask friends or family to be in your videos. Be creative! Check out other company videos on Instagram and TikTok, then have fun making your own! ⓚ

Did You Know?

The most popular form of advertising online is video marketing.

Design Your Own Advertisement

Did You Know?

Have you ever stopped to look at the time on a person's watch in an advertisement? It is usually set to 10:10 because the watch's hands frame the name of the brand and it makes a smiley face.

MARKETING
smarts

What Is Product Placement?

Product placement is when a company pays money to put their product in a movie or TV show. A company does this to get people to buy their product. Have you ever seen your favorite actor drink a brand of soda on TV and then decide that you also want to have that soda? That is product placement! You can use product placement to help sell your product, too. If you are making T-shirts, you can ask some of your friends to wear them. When other people see your friends wearing the T-shirts, it may make them want to buy one of your T-shirts so they can wear one, too.

Do I Need to Offer a Discount?

Coupons are another tool that companies use to get people to buy their product by offering a discount. You can offer coupons that give customers a small discount when they try your product or service. It's important to remember that the whole point of having your own business is to make money so if you do offer a coupon, make sure you are not giving too much of a discount.

What Is a Slogan and Do I Need One for My Business?

A **slogan** is a catchy saying that companies use to get people to buy their product. A slogan is usually something short and clever. When a company uses a slogan, it is just another way to advertise. It isn't something that you have to have for your business. As the business owner, you get to decide if you want to come up with one.

How Should I Advertise?

It depends on your business and the customers that you are trying to reach. This goes back to the market research you did earlier. Do you think your customers will look at the flyers that you hand out? Or do you think they'll throw them away? Do you think your customers will read your e-mail or social media posts? This is something that only you can decide after you do your market research. **K**

buy now!

DREAMING ABOUT
advertising

If you could make a video or commercial to advertise your business, what would it be about? Who would be in your video? Would you show it on social media? What would it be like to film it?

FIND THE *hidden message*

Use the clues to find the hidden message within the boxes below.

1.	2.	3.	4.	5.	6.	7.	8.	9.	10.	11.	12.
B	D	X	U	C	I	U	P	N	M	Q	L
C	A	T	B	S	W	Z	Q	T	K	U	P
A	T	V	C	R	P	I	S	E	C	Z	U
S	N	A	R	T	T	F	C	B	U	Y	J
G	F	B	J	V	M	J	N	O	X	S	D

1. Cross out all the vowels in columns 2, 4, 6, and 12.
2. Find all the letters on the corners and cross them out.
3. Change all the Js to Rs and circle them.
4. Cross out the second letter in columns 4 through 10 and in column 12.
5. Cross out the last letters in columns 2, 3, 5, 6, 8, 9, 10, and 11.
6. Change all the Cs to Es and circle them.
7. Cross out all the letters found in the word **ADVERTISE** in columns 1 through 9.

8. Cross out all the letters found in the phrase **START UP** in columns 1 through 5 and columns 7 and 8.
9. Cross out all the letters in columns 9, 10, and 11 that spell out the word **BUY.**
10. Cross out the first letter in box 3, the fourth letter in box 7, the first letter in box 10, and the first and third letter in box 11.
11. There will be one letter left in each column. Circle each one, and then put each letter in the answer boxes. What is the secret message?

ANSWER KEY ON PAGE 59

ADVICE FROM KID ENTREPRENEURS WHO'VE MADE OVER...
a million dollars!

There's no age limit when it comes to being a millionaire these days, and a handful of kids have struck it rich. These cool kids are small business owners, inventors, and entrepreneurs. Let's meet six kids who made a million, or more!

Evan of EvanTube

With the help of his dad, this 8-year-old launched his own YouTube channel, titled EvanTube, and rakes in about $1.3 million each year. He reviews toys, talks about things that other kids are into, and he's got an audience that will grow with him. There are quite a few YouTube millionaires, so if you can pull it off, it's a free way to create your own brand.

Christian Owens

Christian Owens made his first million at the age of 16. He got his own computer as a kid and taught himself web design in middle school. By the age of 14, he'd started his own design company. Founder of Mac Bundle Box, he negotiated with developers and manufacturers to offer simple, discounted packages for his customers.

Adam Hildreth

When he was just 14, Adam Hildreth got together with friends to create Dubit—a social networking site. It was wildly popular in the United Kingdom and by his sixteenth birthday he had nearly $3.7 million in the bank.

Cameron Johnson

Cameron Johnson was asked by his parents to make invitations for a neighborhood party when he was 11. The guests liked the cards and started paying him to make cards for them. He started the business "Cheers and Tears" and by the time he was 14, he moved on to online advertising and software development. By high school, his monthly income was around $400,000.

Emil Motycka

What started as a lawn-mowing business when he was 9 turned into Motycka Enterprises by the time he was 18. In order to keep up with all the demands of being a teenager, Emil often works the night shift.

Ryan of "Ryan's Barkery"

Featured on *Shark Tank* as an elementary school kid, Ryan raked in $25,000 for selling 25 percent of his business. At 12 years old, Ryan is a young entrepreneur and founder of a dog treat bakery.

Think you can't make a million? Think again. If these kids can do it, so can you! Ⓚ

LAUNCHING A BUSINESS
resources

Biz Kid$
- bizkids.com/resources/

Girls with Ideas
- girlswithideas.com/blog/2017/6/
  20/entrepreneurship-resources-
  for-kids

Entrepreneur Kids
- entrepreneur.com/kids

Kidpreneurs with Big Ideas
- kidpreneurs.org/a-guide-to-50-
  creative-business-ideas-for-kids/

Shopify
- shopify.com/entrepreneur/kids

Teaching Kids Business.Com
- teachingkidsbusiness.com

puzzle solutions

Crack The Business Code page 11

THE SECRET TO

GETTING AHEAD IS

GETTING STARTED.

— MARK TWAIN

Crossword page 30

Across:
4. RESEARCH
5. COMPETITION
6. SUCCESS
7. GOOD
9. SERVICE

Down:
1. PRODUCT
2. IDEA
3. BUSINESS
5. CUSTOMER
8. NAME

Word Search page 12

```
B W E G D R E A M F B E
L J N S G Q W P M M P S
L K T C N V N Y R O O I
U S R H I L Y O O N S H
F I E E D M S D S E S C
S R P D E A S U T Y I N
S L R U A R E C E S B A
E A E L P B N T V O I R
C O N E A W I I E J L F
C G E D B L S U N Q I V
U S U O M E R U E S T Z
S R N I D B Z H E Y B
```

Hidden Message page 55

ENTREPRENEUR

puzzle solutions

Broken Words Message page 38

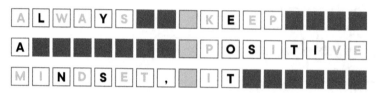

A L W A Y S ■ ■ ░ K E E P ■ ■ ■ ■
A ■ ■ ■ ■ ■ ■ ░ P O S I T I V E
M I N D S E T , ░ I T ■ ■ ■ ■ ■ ■

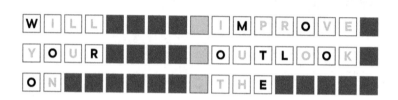

W I L L ■ ■ ■ ░ I M P R O V E ■
Y O U R ■ ■ ■ ░ O U T L O O K ■
O N ■ ■ ■ ■ ■ ░ T H E ■ ■ ■ ■

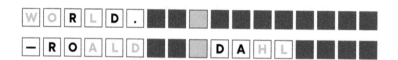

W O R L D . ■ ■ ░ ■ ■ ■ ■ ■ ■ ■
— R O A L D ■ ■ ░ D A H L ■ ■ ■

Word Search page 45

```
A H J E T A E R C Z O S
G N I T E K R A M L Q A
L L E S N Y B R G O R S
I N R A B Z O U A G Y R
N L M F W V L L G O O D
R E M O T S U C P K Z V
F N A L P A J Y I M T D
A P R O D U C T G X E F
Q C O M P E T I T I O N
H Z H C R A E S E R R Q
G Q K Y N A P M O C V U
S E I L P P U S K R O W
```

Maze page 45

CPSIA information can be obtained
at www.ICGtesting.com
Printed in the USA
JSHW031459200521
14888JS00001B/4